the OTHER COAST

the OTHER COAST

ROAD RAGE IN BEVERLY HILLS

by Adrian Raeside

Andrews McMeel
Publishing

Kansas City

The Other Coast is syndicated by Creators Syndicate. For information, write Creators Syndicate, 5777 W. Century Blvd., Suite 700, Los Angeles, CA 90045.

For information, write Andrews McMeel Publishing, an Andrews McMeel Universal company, 4520 Main Street, Kansas City, Missouri 64111.

04 05 06 07 08 BBG 10 9 8 7 6 5 4 3 2 1

ISBN: 0-7407-4668-5

Library of Congress Control Number: 2004103568

the OTHER COAST
RAESIDE
I TELL YOU SON. STICK WITH ME AND I'LL TEACH YOU EVERYTHING THERE IS TO KNOW ABOUT FALLING TREES.
OB'S TREES

YOU NEED A GOOD KNOWLEDGE OF PHYSICS AND TRIGONOMETRY.
BIOLOGY HELPS, AS WELL AS THE ABILITY TO RUN FAST.
WHY DO I HAVE TO BE ABLE TO RUN FAST?
FOR WHEN THE TREE FALLS THE WRONG WAY.

LET'S SEE... WHAT WILL I BE TODAY?
COUNTRY, OR ROCK AND ROLL?
RAESIDE
HOW ABOUT FRUSTRATED WRITER WITH LITTLE TALENT?
RACKED WITH TUBERCULOSIS, OR SUICIDAL ALCOHOLIC?

RAESIDE
IF HEMINGWAY COULD WRITE BRILLIANT NOVELS ON A TYPEWRITER, SO CAN I.

VICKY, WHERE DO I PLUG IN THE WIRELESS CARD?
TYPEWRITERS WERE PRE-WIRELESS, TOULOSE.
OH, OF COURSE, IT'S DIAL-UP.

O.K. TYPEWRITER, WORK YOUR HEMINGWAY MAGIC!

RAESIDE
I'M GOING OUT TO FIND A BULLFIGHT.

WHAT THE 'E' IN E-BUSINESS STANDS FOR:
TOTAL SALES
$0000
EEEEEEE EEEEEE!!
RAESIDE

ALRIGHT! MY FIVE HUNDREDTH REJECTION LETTER AND I'VE FINALLY GOT A BOOK!
SNAILS FOUND ON MARS!
RAESIDE

THAT'S GREAT. I CAN'T WAIT TO SEE IT PUBLISHED.
DOG ELEC
VICE-PRES
CORPORATI

500 REJECTIONS
A COLLECTION OF 500 REJECTION LETTERS.

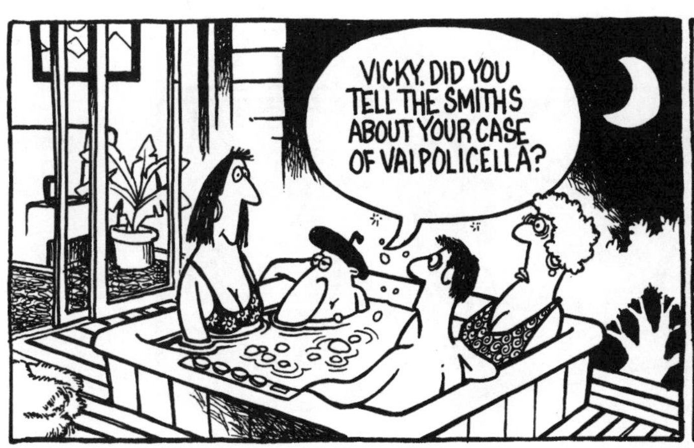
VICKY, DID YOU TELL THE SMITHS ABOUT YOUR CASE OF VALPOLICELLA?

RAESIDE
THAT'S A WINE, YOU IDIOTS!

the OTHER COAST
EVEN THOUGH I'M AT THE BEACH, I CAN'T GET WORK OFF MY MIND.

RAESIDE
YOU'RE GOING ABOUT IT THE WRONG WAY, MAN. YOU SHOULD DO WHAT I DO...
EVERY SUNNY DAY, I DROP EVERYTHING I'M DOING AT NOON AND HEAD TO THE BEACH. REGARDLESS OF WHAT'S HAPPENING AT WORK.
I DON'T TAKE THE CELL PHONE AND I DON'T TELL ANYONE WHERE I AM.
HOW DOES YOUR EMPLOYER FEEL ABOUT THIS?
DUNNO. THEY FIRED ME.

I HATE WORKING IN THIS CUBICLE. I FEEL ALONE AND ISOLATED FROM MY CO-WORKERS.

RAESIDE

YEAH... UH-HUH... OK... YEP... UH-HUH...

THESE TECH SUPPORT GEEKS SEEM TO SPEAK A LANGUAGE ALL OF THEIR OWN.

TECH SUPPORT
RAESIDE

YECCH! YOU LOOK TERRIBLE! WHAT HAPPENED TO YOU?
YOU KNOW THAT HOME BREW WINE KIT I BOUGHT LAST MONTH?
RAESIDE

I DRANK OVER HALF OF IT LAST NIGHT. AND NOW I FEEL LIKE A GIANT, BUBBLING TUB OF SLUDGE...

HOW LONG DID YOU FERMENT IT?
FERMENT?

RAESIDE
HOMEMADE WINE COMPETITION
AAAH...THE DELICATE AROMA OF GYM SOCKS AND THE CHEEKY TASTE OF A GORILLA'S ARMPIT, COMBINING TO CREATE A VICIOUS, HEAD-POUNDING FINISH.

I HAVE TO SAY VICKY, THIS IS THE BEST PIECE OF FANTASY I'VE EVER WRITTEN.
RAESIDE
SCI-FI?
TAX RETURN.

HERE IT GOES...A TWENTY FIVE PAGE LETTER TO THE EDITOR.
KA-CHUNK
DON'T STAPLE IT TOULOSE!
RAESIDE
WHY?
STAPLES JAM THE PAPER SHREDDER.

the OTHER COAST
BUFFET
ALL U CAN EAT $5.

RAESIDE
OH NOOO... IT'S LARRY.

ALL YOU CAN EAT- $5.00

URP!

ORDERING MORE FOOD?
DECLARING CHAPTER ELEVEN.

WHY DIDN'T WE PUBLISH YOUR LETTER? WELL, IT WAS LIBELOUS...
EDITOR

IN BAD TASTE, OVER 200 WORDS LONG...
RAESIDE

AND WRITTEN IN RED CRAYON ON THE BACK OF A BAR COASTER.
WHAT IF I DOUBLE-SPACED IT?
EDITOR

WOW! YOU'VE GOT A GREAT STORY HERE.
AGENT

THE MAIN CHARACTER IS SUCH A SAD, PATHETIC LOSER! THIS IS ONE OF THE BEST SCRIPT TREATMENTS I'VE EVER READ!

RAESIDE
THAT'S MY RESUMÉ.

SO I HEARD BACK FROM THE STUDIO. THEY LOVE THE SCRIPT, BUT WANT TO MAKE SOME TINY CHANGES.
HOLLYWOO
RAESIDE

We're dumping everything except the title.
HOLLYWOOD -ENGLISH DICTIONARY

AUTO PART
THIS IS OUR BEST CAR ALARM. IT'S GUARANTEED THEFT-PROOF.

GREAT. GO AHEAD AND INSTALL IT IN MY CAR.

BEEP!
ONE HOUR LATER:
RAESIDE

COSMETICS
OH YES, IT'S QUITE SAFE. WE TEST ALL OUR PRODUCTS ON HUMANS FIRST.
RAESIDE

EVEN WALKING TO THE CANDY MACHINE LEFT ME OUT OF BREATH. SO I'M CHANGING MY LIFESTYLE.
GOOD FOR YOU LARRY. YOU BOUGHT A GYM MEMBERSHIP?

NOPE. I BOUGHT A SCOOTER.
RAESIDE

the OTHER COAST
TECH SERVICE

HELLO TOULOSE? I'VE DISCOVERED WHY YOUR KEYBOARD FROZE UP.
IT WAS ATTACKED BY A FRUIT-BASED, ORGANIC VIRUS.
RAESIDE
SOUNDS SERIOUS. WHAT IS IT?
THE REMAINS OF A JELLY DONUT.

I SEE YOU'RE RE-CHARGING YOUR SCOOTER IN YOUR CUBICLE.
IS THAT A PROBLEM?
NOT IF YOU UNPLUG IT.
RAESIDE

WHERE'S YOUR SCOOTER, LARRY?
IN THE SHOP. I'M GETTING IT CAMPERIZED.
RAESIDE
LATER:
THAT'S CAMPERIZED?
CHECK OUT THE DRINK HOLDER.

OFF FOR LUNCH AT THE DONUT STORE?
SINCE I GOT THIS SCOOTER, I'VE NOT SET FOOT IN A FAST FOOD RESTAURANT.
RAESIDE
I USE THE DRIVE-THRU INSTEAD.
ORDER HERE

VICKY, SOMEONE STOLE MY SCOOTER LAST NIGHT.
GOOD. IT WAS DUMB.
BUT THE COPS CAUGHT THE GUY.
LOW SPEED HIGHWAY CHASE?
SPIKE BELT ACROSS THE ROAD.
RAESIDE

FURTHER PROOF OF THE IMPACT OF T.V. SEX & VIOLENCE ON SOCIETY:
BANK
RAESIDE

WHEN MILK GOES BAD...
2%
MILK
CLOSE THE DOOR FATSO! THE LAST THING YOU NEED IS ANOTHER SNACK!
RAESIDE

the OTHER COAST
YOUR DIGITAL NETWORK HUB IS HERE.
RECEPTIO

RAESIDE
SIGN THIS WAYBILL IN TRIPLICATE.
I NEED YOU TO SIGN THIS REQUISITION FOR PAYMENT.
PHOTOCOPY THE MANUAL AND FILL OUT THE WARRANTY FORMS.
WHAT DOES THIS DO?
HUB
CUTS DOWN OFFICE PAPER.

RAESIDE
I SEE IT'S GOING TO BE A COLD WINTER TOULOSE.
HOW CAN YOU TELL? WOOLLY CATERPILLARS? GEESE FLYING SOUTH?
THE NEIGHBORS ARE STEALING OUR FIREWOOD.

Happiness is:....
RAESIDE
SUV 4x4

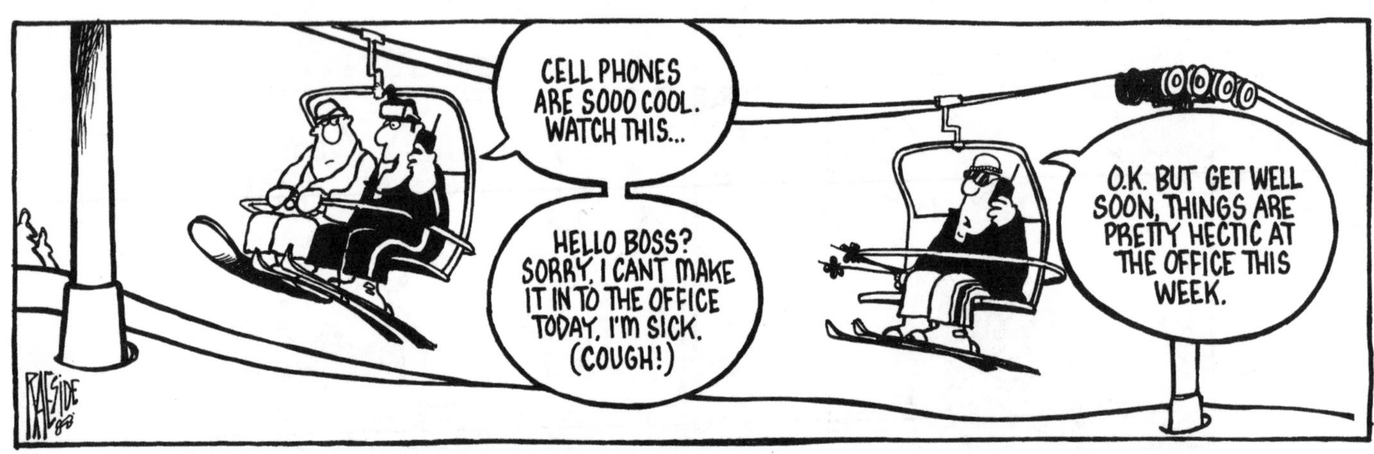
CELL PHONES ARE SOOO COOL. WATCH THIS...
HELLO BOSS? SORRY, I CANT MAKE IT IN TO THE OFFICE TODAY, I'M SICK. (COUGH!)
O.K. BUT GET WELL SOON, THINGS ARE PRETTY HECTIC AT THE OFFICE THIS WEEK.
RAESIDE

GLADYS' SON BOBBY HAS LANDED A ROLE IN A NEW T.V. SERIES.
BOBBY? HE'S A TALENTLESS OAF!
RAESIDE

IT'S A REALITY SERIES.
A STAR IS BORN.

MOVIE STARS HAVE BEEN DISCOVERED IN MALT SHOPS, T.V. STARS IN HIGHSCHOOL PLAYS...
WHERE DO THEY DISCOVER REALITY T.V. PLAYERS?
RAESIDE

SURE, I'D EAT A SLUG FOR A CHANCE TO MARRY A MILLIONAIRE...
UNDER ROCKS.

AMAZING MR. FARNSWORTH, YOU'VE INVENTED TELEVISION! JUST IMAGINE ITS USES. SITCOMS, REALITY SHOWS...

RAESIDE
KA-BLAM!

the OTHER COAST
LOOK. WILDFLOWERS!

RAESIDE
AREN'T THEY GORGEOUS?
SO FRAGILE, SO TENDER.
AN EXPLOSION OF COLOUR AND FRAGRANCE!
ISN'T NATURE WONDERFUL.

AIEEE! SPLASH SPLASH!
OHMIGOSH! TO WIN IMMUNITY, THE TEAMS ARE SWIMMING THROUGH AN ALLIGATOR INFESTED SWAMP.
WHO WON?
BURP!
THE ALLIGATORS.
RAESIDE

EEEUW! RED TEAM HAS TO CRAWL THROUGH A DITCH FILLED WITH WRITHING WORMS.
RAESIDE
HOW HUMILIATING.
YEAH. THE WORMS WILL SPEND MONTHS IN PSYCHOTHERAPY.

acting classes for reality T.V. players:
O.K. STAND THERE AND LOOK LIKE IDIOTS.
PERFECT! PICK UP YOUR DIPLOMAS ON YOUR WAY OUT.
RAESIDE

RAESIDE
I JUST HARVESTED HIM FOR 'SCIENTIFIC PURPOSES.'

VICKY, WE HAVE THE MOST ADVANCED COMPUTER SYSTEMS SECURITY AVAILABLE.
YET YOU CAN'T GET ME A STATUS REPORT. SOMEONE HACKED OUR SYSTEM?
SOMEONE SWIPED MY COMPUTER.
RAESIDE

RAESIDE
I SUPPOSE IT WAS INEVITABLE AS THE BABY BOOMERS AGED...
EXIT 20

the OTHER COAST

GOOD EVENING. HAVE YOU GIVEN ANY THOUGHT TO THE FUTURE?
UH... SOMETIMES.
THEN YOU'LL BE INTERESTED IN THIS AMAZING LIFE INSURANCE AND MAGAZINE OFFER!
COMPANY
IN SPACE NO ONE CAN HEAR YOU SCREAM.
RJESIDE

THERE'S A SUSPICIOUS-LOOKING CHARACTER...

OHMIGOSH! HE JUST PILFERED A LAPTOP.

THAT MAN IS A THIEF! CALL SECURITY!
SIR, HE IS SECURITY.
RAESIDE

I GUESS I SHOULD BE HAPPY OUR CORPORATE PHILOSOPHY HAS FILTERED DOWN TO ALL DEPARTMENTS.

AARGH! I'M IN A DEAD END JOB!
C'MON VICKY, TRY DOING STAN, THE INTER-OFFICE MAIL BOY'S JOB.

WHAT'S SO DEAD END ABOUT HIS JOB, LARRY?

INTER-OFFICE MAIL HAS BEEN ELECTRONIC FOR TWO YEARS.
RAESIDE

VICKY, HAVE YOU SEEN KEN IN SALES?
HE'S ON THE ROAD, LARRY.

THAT'S COOL. TORONTO? NEW YORK? SEATTLE?

NO, THE ROAD. HE WAS FIRED THIS MORNING.
GRABBIT and RUNNE
RAESIDE

I GET THE FEELING MOTHER NATURE DOESN'T SHARE YOUR ENTHUSIASM FOR FOUR WHEEL DRIVING.
WHAT MAKES YOU THINK THAT, TOULOSE?
YOU'RE PARKED ON HER.
RAESIDE

RAESIDE
LARRY, I FAIL TO SEE HOW SITTING IN TWO TONS OF AIR CONDITIONED LUXURY CAN BE CONSIDERED RECREATION.
I'VE GOT A HOME GYM SET UP IN THE BACK.

SO, YOU WENT OFF-ROAD AND ENCOUNTERED A RABBIT, TWO SQUIRRELS AND A RACCOON.
WOW! HOW CAN YOU TELL?
RAESIDE
THEY'RE STILL STUCK IN YOUR TREADS.

the OTHER COAST

AAAAH... ANOTHER DAY IN THE LIFE OF A CONCERNED ENVIRONMENTALIST.

SHOWER WITH RECYCLED WOOD CHIP SOAP AND SOLAR HEATED WATER.

DRY MY HAIR WITH A HYDROGEN POWERED HAIR DRYER.

SLIP MY FEET INTO GUATAMALAN HEMP SLIPPERS.

TUCK INTO A HEALTHY, ALL NATURAL, HIGH-FIBER BREAKFAST.

ROOTS 'N' BARK

SOY MILK

RAESIDE

THERE ARE TENT CATERPILLARS IN THE OAK TREE.

DO YOU THINK IF I TOOK UP ROLLERBLADING I'D LOOK NINETEEN TOO?

VICKY, YOU'D LOOK LIKE AN IDIOT.
AS LONG AS I LOOKED LIKE A NINETEEN YEAR-OLD IDIOT.
RAESIDE

I'VE NEVER BEEN ON ROLLERBLADES AND I HAVE A POOR SENSE OF BALANCE. IS THERE SOME SORT OF TRAINING I SHOULD TAKE FIRST?
SPORTS
FIRST AID.
RAESIDE

RAESIDE
OOOOOO! I FEEL LIKE I'M NINETEEN!

OOOO... I FEEL LIKE I'M NINETY.
GET WELL SOON

AB-O-FLEX
MASTER
EXERCISE MACHINES ARE A WASTE OF MONEY VICKY. MY GRAMPA WAS THE FITTEST PERSON I KNEW, AND HE NEVER USED MACHINES.
RAESIDE

HE NEVER EVEN DROVE A CAR, PREFERRING TO WALK INSTEAD.

WOW. DID HE LIVE PAST A HUNDRED?
NOPE. SIXTY. DAD BACKED OVER HIM WITH THE CAR WHEN HE WAS DOING PUSHUPS IN THE DRIVEWAY.

INSTRUCTIONS FOR ASSEMBLING YOUR BICEP-FLEX...
ATTACH ARM 'A' TO BASE 'D'... FLEXNUTS... HEX DRIVER... TENSION SPRINGS... BLAH, BLAH
BICEP-FLEX
ASSEMBLY

RAESIDE
WHAT A FRUSTRATING WASTE OF TIME!

HEYYY... IT WORKS.

AIRLINES REMOVING SEATS TO CREATE MORE LEG ROOM IS AN EXCELLENT IDEA.
I WONDER WHICH SEATS WERE REMOVED?

RAESIDE

the OTHER COAST
RAESIDE
WHAT A NOBLE TREE. Y'KNOW IT INSPIRES ME TO WRITE...

The Noble Tree. a novel

PUBLISHIN
THE NOBLE TREE. THIS COULD BE A BLOCKBUSTER.

FIFTY THOUSAND COPIES OF THE NOBLE TREE. WE'RE GOING TO NEED MORE PAPER.

IT WAS THEN THAT PAT REALIZED A SCREW-TOP CHAMPAGNE BOTTLE WOULD HAVE BEEN PREFERABLE...
POP!
SSSSSSSSSSSS
RAESIDE

HOW ARE NEGOTIATIONS GOING?
SO FAR HE'S GOT A BOOK DEAL, A MOVIE OF THE WEEK DEAL AND A RECORDING CONTRACT.
BANK
RAESIDE

MEDICAL ALERT BRACELET FOR OENOPHILES:
ALLERGIES:
1987 merlot, 1992 shiraz,
any zinfandels under $10.
RAESIDE

SPORTS BARS THAT DIDN'T QUITE MAKE IT...
SPORTS BAR
BEER ON TAP
TONITE!
CHESS ON THE BIG SCREEN T.V.
RAESIDE

CHECK THIS OUT VICKY. THE SMALLEST STEREO AND CD PLAYER ON THE MARKET.
SO WHY DOES IT COME IN SUCH A BIG BOX?
THE REMOTE.
RAESIDE

MUGGINGS IN THE CARIBBEAN, PICKPOCKETS IN EUROPE... HOLIDAYS JUST AREN'T SAFE ANYMORE.
YOU'RE RIGHT. LETS STAY HOME AND GET RIPPED OFF BY THE POWER COMPANY, GAS COMPANY AND CABLE COMPANY INSTEAD.
TRAVEL
Z
RAESIDE

the OTHER COAST
SON, IT'S TIME YOU LEARNED OUR FAMILY HISTORY.

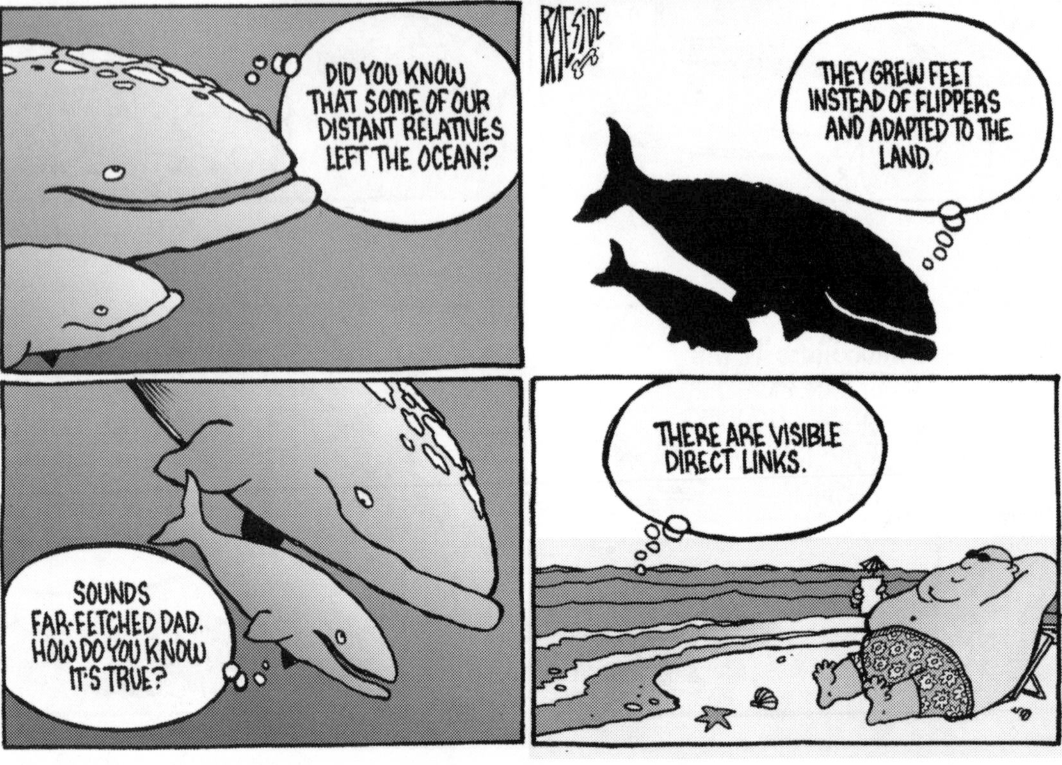

DID YOU KNOW THAT SOME OF OUR DISTANT RELATIVES LEFT THE OCEAN?
BAESIDE
THEY GREW FEET INSTEAD OF FLIPPERS AND ADAPTED TO THE LAND.
SOUNDS FAR-FETCHED DAD. HOW DO YOU KNOW IT'S TRUE?
THERE ARE VISIBLE DIRECT LINKS.

PHYSIOTHERAPIST
LARRY, YOU'VE GOT WEIRD LUMPS IN YOUR BACK.
GYM
Y'KNOW, THEY FEEL LIKE TEETH!
THEY ARE. I USED TO PLAY RUGBY.
RAESIDE

SUSHI
O.K. TIME TO TAKE THE LEFTOVER HOLIDAY TURKEY SUSHI OFF THE MENU.
RAESIDE

EVER BEEN ARRESTED?
EMPLO
ONCE. FOR WEARING PANTYHOSE.
SINCE WHEN IS WEARING PANTYHOSE A CRIME?
WHEN THEY'RE ON YOUR HEAD AND YOU'RE INSIDE A BANK.
RAESIDE

WHY DOGS DON'T PLAY GOLF:
WHACK!

RAESIDE
ARF ARF ARF ARF ARF ARF

THANK GOODNESS YOU'RE HERE. MY HUSBAND HAS BEEN STUCK IN THE ELEVATOR FOR TWO HOURS!
I HOPE WE'RE NOT TOO LATE! WHAT KIND OF MUZAK IS PLAYING?
27
27

SOUNDS LIKE CHRISTMAS CAROLS ON THE PAN FLUTE.
FORGET IT. HE'S A GONER.
RAESIDE

I TOLD YOU IT WAS A MISTAKE TO LET THAT WALL STREET BROKER LOOK AFTER OUR NUTS!
WILL SQUEAK FOR FOOD
RAESIDE

the OTHER COAST
DR. JeKYLL
CITY
20
MILES

RAESIDE

CITY
15
MILES

CITY
10 MILES

CITY
5 MILES

CITY NEXT EXIT

..MR. HYDe
PARK

HONEY, I SHRUNK THE MEAL!
NOW PLAYING
AT A FRENCH RESTAURANT NEAR YOU.
RAESIDE

EVERY YEAR, AS A CEO, I HAVE TO GO BEFORE THE PUBLIC AND MAKE PROMISES I CAN'T KEEP.
TELL ME ABOUT IT.
RAESIDE

ARE YOUR DONUTS FRESH?
YES SIR! THEY'RE MADE FRESH DAILY.
RAESIDE
...IN CHINA.
DONUTS

GAS BILL, ELECTRIC BILL, WATER BILL... AT LEAST AIR IS FREE.
WANNA BET?
CHIPS
RAESIDE

DO YOU PICK UP AFTER YOUR DOG?
YEP. I USE THE RUNNING SHOE METHOD.
RAESIDE
RUNNING SHOE?
ATTACHED TO A JOGGER.

RAESIDE
AND THEY SAY PIGS CAN'T FLY.
CHIPS

the OTHER COAST
RAESIDE
OMIGOSH! SOMEONE DO SOMETHING! MY HUSBAND IS CHOKING!
MENU
MENU
THE PHONE BOOK HAS INSTRUCTIONS ON WHAT TO DO FOR A CHOKING VICTIM!
PHONE
LONG DISTANCE AREA CODES, WIRELESS SERVICES, PAGERS...
TELECONFERENCING INSTRUCTIONS, VIDEO CONFERENCE SERVICES, CALLING CARDS...
EASY ONLINE PAYMENTS, CREDIT ENQUIRIES...
DID YOU FIND HEIMLICH MANEUVER INSTRUCTIONS?
NOPE. JUST WHACKED HIM ON THE BACK WITH THE PHONE BOOK.
MENU
MENU

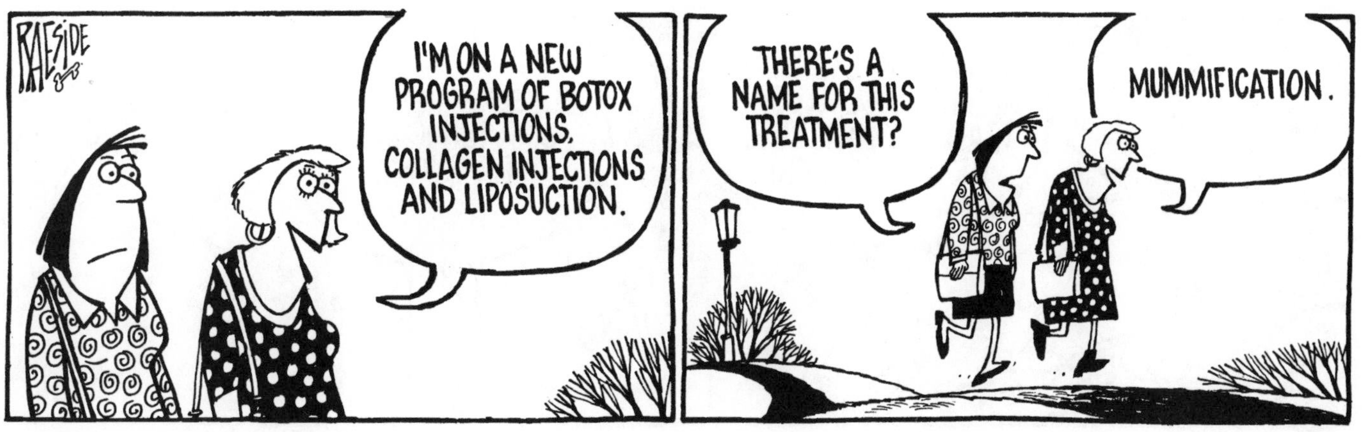
RAESIDE
I'M ON A NEW PROGRAM OF BOTOX INJECTIONS, COLLAGEN INJECTIONS AND LIPOSUCTION.
THERE'S A NAME FOR THIS TREATMENT?
MUMMIFICATION.

I LOVE THE CHANGING SEASONS IN MAINE. SUMMER, FALL... WHAT'S THE SEASON ON THE COAST, VICKY?
RAESIDE
MUDSLIDE.

WHAT A MUDSLIDE! OUR PATIO FURNITURE IS MISSING...
RAESIDE
THE CAR, THE TOOL SHED...
WHAT ELSE IS MISSING, TOULOSE?
OUR INSURANCE ADJUSTER.

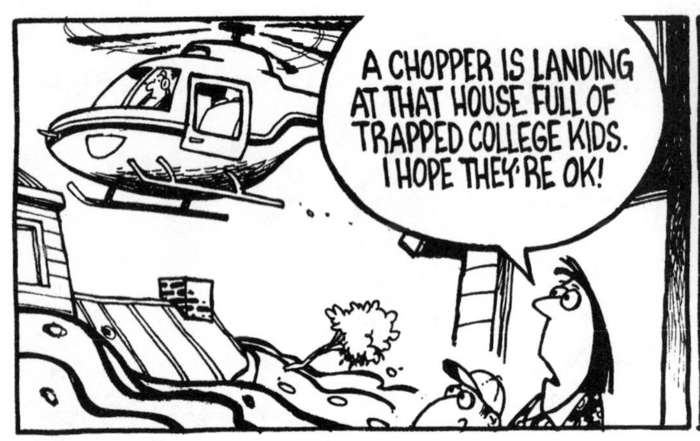
A CHOPPER IS LANDING AT THAT HOUSE FULL OF TRAPPED COLLEGE KIDS. I HOPE THEY'RE OK!

RELAX. THEY'RE JUST FLYING OUT THEIR EMPTIES.
RAESIDE

RAESIDE
WE'RE CUT OFF BY A MUDSLIDE WITH NO OUTSIDE HELP. WE'LL STARVE!
RELAX VICKY, I SENT OUT FOR PIZZA.
PIZZA

THE PIZZA DELIVERY GUY CAN GET THROUGH BUT THE FIRE TRUCKS CAN'T?
EVER TIPPED A FIREMAN?
PIZZA

TOULOSE, WHAT'S THE WORST THING ABOUT BEING TRAPPED IN A MUDSLIDE? THE ISOLATION? THE LONELINESS?
RAESIDE
WHUP! WHUP!

TV
TV
THE NOISE.

the OTHER COAST
OMIGOSH! THAT'S A HIDEOUS, BLOOD-CURDLING SOUND.
WHAT KIND OF TORTURED SOUL COULD EMIT SUCH A TERRIFYING CRY?
SOME HIDEOUS EVENT MUST HAVE LEFT A TERRIBLE IMPRINT ON THIS ENTITY...

AND IT CAN ONLY BE ONE THING...
KLIK
RAESIDE

TOULOSE, HOW MANY TIMES HAVE I TOLD YOU, STOP CHECKING OUR MUTUAL FUNDS!

GEE DOC, WITH SOARING MALPRACTICE PREMIUMS, HOW CAN YOU AFFORD TO KEEP YOUR CLINIC OPEN?
I'M EXPLORING ALTERNATE REVENUE SOURCES.
RAESIDE

WHAT A DARLING LAWN ORNAMENT! HOW MUCH?
YOU CAN HAVE HIM FOR A DOLLAR.
ANTIQUES
RAESIDE
WHY SO CHEAP?
HE'S MY HUSBAND.
Scratch Scratch
ANTIQUES

LARRY, EATING MEAT EXPOSES YOU TO DISEASES LIKE MAD COW AND BIRD FLU. AS A VEGAN, I'M NOT EXPOSED TO THOSE KIND OF RISKS.
JEEPERS SIMON, WHAT HAPPENED TO YOU?
DUTCH ELM DISEASE.
RAESIDE

RAESIDE
SO SAD. THE GIANT GOPHER IS NOW ON THE ENDANGERED LIST. I WONDER WHY?
WILDLIFE
GOPHER
GOPHER GYOZAS
GOPHER PIE
FROZEN GIANT GOPHER STRIPS
GIANT GOPHER mm mm GOOD! HELPER
GOPHER FONDUE

RAESIDE
HUNTED ALMOST TO EXTINCTION, THE GIANT GOPHER IS EASILY IDENTIFIED BY UNIQUE MARKINGS ON HIS BACK.

RAESIDE
NEW SHOES VICKY?
SHOE SHACK

I'M WEARING THEM AT THE ENDANGERED GIANT GOPHER FUNDRAISER.

MADE FROM 100% GIANT GOPHER HIDE

the OTHER COAST
OH NO! THEY'RE GOING TO PAVE THAT EMPTY LOT!
BOBS PAVING

DON'T YOU REALIZE THE VALUE OF GREEN SPACE?
WITHOUT GREEN SPACE, THIS PLANET WOULD DIE!
RAESIDE
RELAX, WE PLAN ON MAKING THIS PARKING LOT ENVIRONMENTALLY FRIENDLY.
THEY PAINTED THE PARKING STRIPES GREEN?
THEY DID USE LEAD-FREE PAINT.

COCKTAIL FUNDRAISER FOR THE ENDANGERED GIANT GOPHER, COCKTAIL FUND-RAISER FOR THE PANDA.
COCKTAIL FUNDRAISER FOR THE ENDANGERED SNAIL-DARTER.
RAESIDE

AM I MISSING ANY EVENTS?
A FUNDRAISER FOR YOUR ENDANGERED LIVER?

HEY VICKY, THE GIANT GOPHER IS BEING FEATURED IN A T.V. PROGRAM.
I TOLD YOU I COULD RAISE INTEREST IN THE ENDANGERED GIANT GOPHER!

LIGHTLY BASTE THE MEAT...
IT'S A COOKING SHOW.
RAESIDE

NOTHING LIKE A SWANK FUNDRAISER FOR RAISING AWARENESS ABOUT ENDANGERED SPECIES.
SPOTTED OWL NIBBLIES?
RAESIDE

SPOTTED OWL NIBBLIES?
WOULD MADAM PREFER WHOOPING CRANE KEBABS INSTEAD?

I FOUND THIS COFFEE MUG INFESTED WITH FUNGUS AND MUSHROOMS IN THE LUNCH ROOM 'FRIDGE!
PUT IT BACK LARRY. IT'S SIMON THE VEGAN'S LUNCH.
RAESIDE

GENEALOGY
LARRY, MY RESEARCH PROVES YOU HAD AN ANCESTOR THAT WAS ON THE MAYFLOWER.
GENEALOGY
AS A BARNACLE.
RAESIDE

I WOULDN'T RECOMMEND THIS MATTRESS. IT'S SO LUMPY, NO ONE EVER SLEEPS A SECOND NIGHT ON IT.
WE'LL TAKE IT.
RAESIDE
WE'RE FURNISHING THE GUEST BEDROOM.
SPROING

the OTHER COAST
YOU KNOW SON, THERE WAS A TIME WHEN THIS FOREST WAS HUGE...
A VAST TRACT OF UNSPOILED LAND THAT WENT ON AS FAR AS THE EYE COULD SEE.
NOW WE'RE CONFINED TO A SMALL STRIP OF PRESERVE.
SO WHAT HAPPENED, DAD?
CLEARCUTTING.
RAESIDE

AW, YOU GUYS... YOU REMEMBERED MY BIRTHDAY!
RAESIDE

IT'S AN OFF-LEASH PARK FOR HUMANS.
SINGLES BAR
RAESIDE

I SPEND ALL HALLOWEEN HARRASSING, ANNOYING AND BOTHERING FOLKS.
THE REST OF THE YEAR, I'M A TELEMARKETER.
RAESIDE

THIS BREAKFAST CEREAL IS 100% NATURAL AND HAS AN ENVIRONMENTALLY FRIENDLY TOY INSIDE.
LEAVES 'N' OATS

A LOGGING TRUCK?
WITH A TINY ACTIVIST YOU CAN CHAIN TO IT.
RAESIDE

I LOVE WATCHING DOG SHOWS. WE SHOULD GET A DOG. VICKY.
HOWL!
ARF! ARF!
AROOOOOOO!

YOU'RE WATCHING THE JERRY SPRINGER SHOW.
THINK THEY'RE HOUSE TRAINABLE?
BARK!
RAESIDE

OFF TO ANOTHER ENVIRONMENTAL PROTEST?
YEP. I'M OFF TO PROTEST AN OIL SPILL.
STOP THE SPILL

RAESIDE
YOU COULD START WITH THE DRIVEWAY.

the OTHER COAST
SOUNDS LIKE A PLUGGED DRAIN.

THIS SOUNDS LIKE A DRUNK BULL MOOSE.

TWO TOMCATS FIGHTING ON A TIN ROOF...

RAESIDE
...TWO TOMCATS FIGHTING IN A PLUGGED DRAIN...

NICE WORK GUYS! YOU'VE GOT ENOUGH TRACKS FOR AN ALBUM.

AWW NUTS! THIS NEW WORD PROCESSING SOFTWARE IS AT IT AGAIN!
WHAT'S IT DOING TOULOSE?
EVERY TIME I TYPE A PARAGRAPH IN MY NEW NOVEL, IT FREEZES AND TOSSES IT IN THE TRASH.
COMPUTERS ARE GETTING MORE HUMAN EVERY DAY.

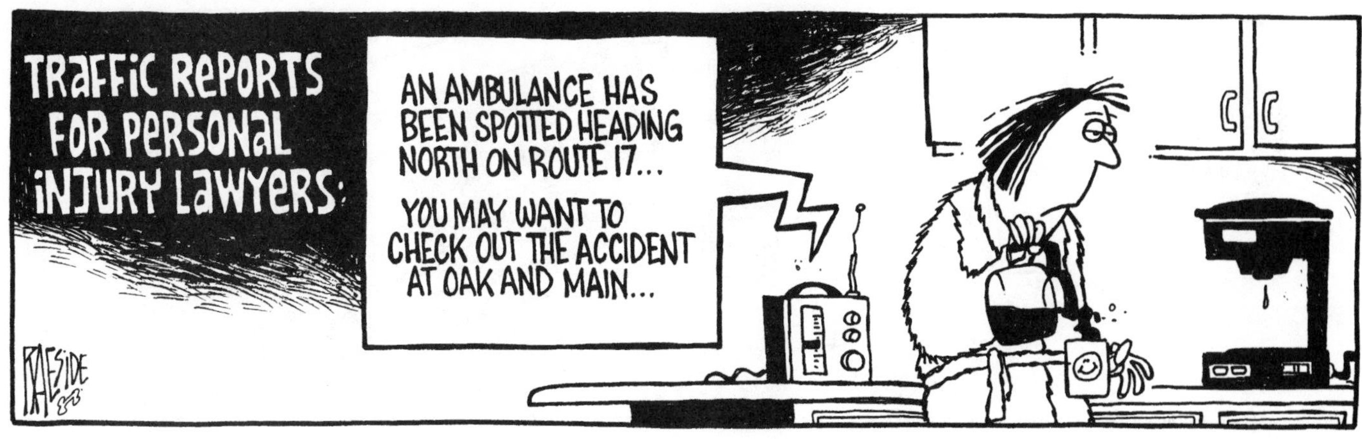
TRAFFIC REPORTS FOR PERSONAL INJURY LAWYERS:
AN AMBULANCE HAS BEEN SPOTTED HEADING NORTH ON ROUTE 17...
YOU MAY WANT TO CHECK OUT THE ACCIDENT AT OAK AND MAIN...

WILDLIFE MODELS?
ROLE MODELS.

RAESIDE
OMIGOSH! THAT NEW LAWYER IS IN THE PARKING LOT, LOCKED IN A DEATH-STRUGGLE WITH AN ALLIGATOR.
CALL 911!
NAH. CALL THE VET.

RAESIDE
I GUESS CHILDHOOD OBESITY REALLY IS BECOMING A PROBLEM.
SCHOOL BUS

RAESIDE
WE TURN UP WITHIN TWENTY FOUR HOURS OF YOUR ALARM GOING OFF.
SECURITY
SECURITY
24 HOUR RESPONSE

the OTHER COAST
DSX5 701

Satellite Delivery:
S
A
$20,000,000.

Satellite Deployment:
$5,000,000.

UPLINK TRUCK:
W-URGH
TELEVISION
$250,000.

RAESIDE
Television Camera:
$50,000.

CONTENT:
TONIGHT, PARTY BALLOONS. CAN THEY CAUSE ROAD RAGE?
WORTHLESS.

RAESIDE
MOUNTAIN BIKES
I'VE GOT THE BEST PRICES. BEST SERVICE AND BEST BIKES, BUT BUSINESS STINKS. WHAT AM I MISSING?
MOUNTAINS.

GOTTA LOVE HYDROPONICALLY GROWN PRODUCE. NO BUGS, NO MOLD, NO BLEMISHES...
NOTASTE.
RAESIDE

RAESIDE
SPEEDING UP THE PROCESS.

IF THE AIRLINES OPERATED THE ARK:
WE APOLOGIZE FOR YOUR CONTINUING TO WAIT. BUT YOUR VOYAGE HAS BEEN DELAYED AGAIN.
RAESIDE

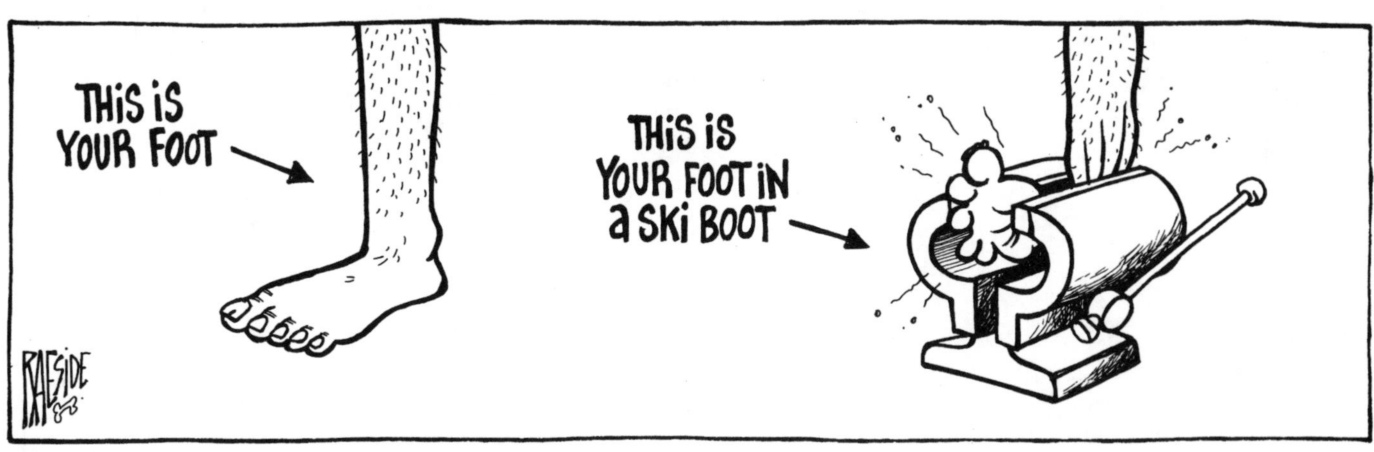
THIS IS YOUR FOOT
THIS IS YOUR FOOT IN A SKI BOOT
RAESIDE

HEH HEH. I JUST SPRAYPAINTED A LADY WEARING A FUR COAT.
RAESIDE
THUS RELEASING CFC'S INTO THE ATMOSPHERE, DEPLETING THE OZONE LAYER.
PERFECT. THE SUN WILL BURN THE FUR OFF HER BACK.

the OTHER COAST

RAESIDE
TOULOSE, YOU'LL BE AMAZED AT THE THINGS USED IN JAPANESE CUISINE.

FOR EXAMPLE, THIS IS NORI, DRIED SEAWEED.
UGH.

OR WASHI, RICE PAPER.
ICK.

MM. WHAT'S THIS?
SEQYUSHO.
DE-LICIOUS! WHAT'S IT CALLED IN ENGLISH?

THE BILL.
P-TOO!

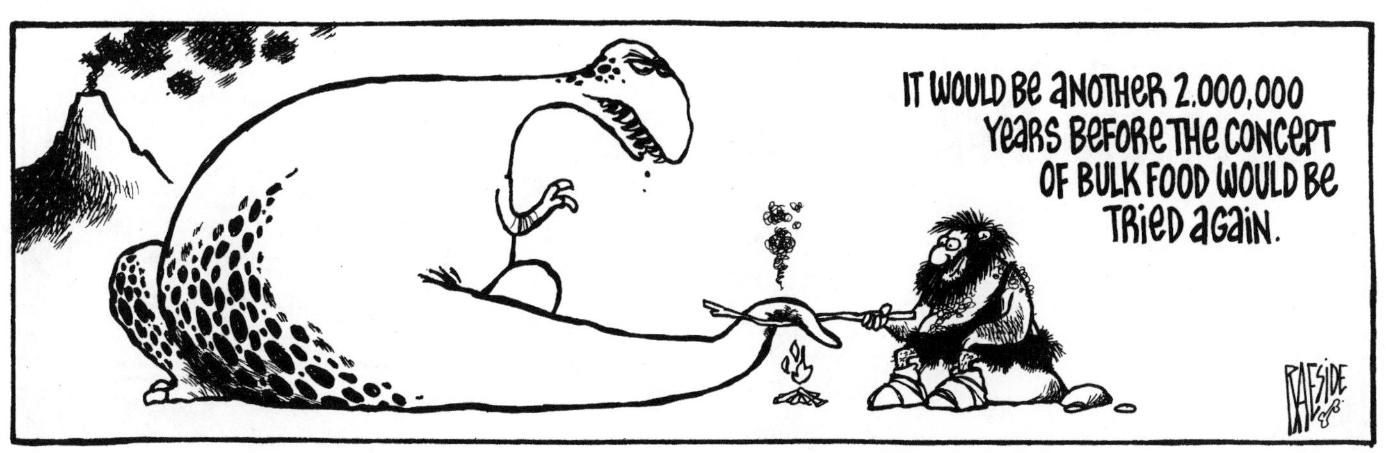
IT WOULD BE ANOTHER 2,000,000 YEARS BEFORE THE CONCEPT OF BULK FOOD WOULD BE TRIED AGAIN.
RAESIDE

WHY THEY'RE CALLED CARPENTER ANTS:
WHOOAH! IT'S ALREADY 3 PM... PACK UP AND LET'S GO HOME.
RAESIDE

THE DOWN-SIDE TO USING AN EXTENSION MIKE & EARPIECE ON YOUR CELLULAR PHONE:
RAESIDE
HE WAS SITTING AT THAT TABLE, TALKING TO HIMSELF FOR OVER TWO HOURS.
CAFÉ

CONTRACTOR COLLEGE
ANNOUNCEMENTS
MID TERM EXAMS
10 AM WEDNESDAY, OR 1 PM.
PERHAPS FRIDAY. BUT
MORE LIKELY NEXT WEEK.
RAESIDE

DINER
HEY, THIS GLASS IS FILTHY!
RAESIDE
DINER
THAT'S JUST YOUR REFLECTION.

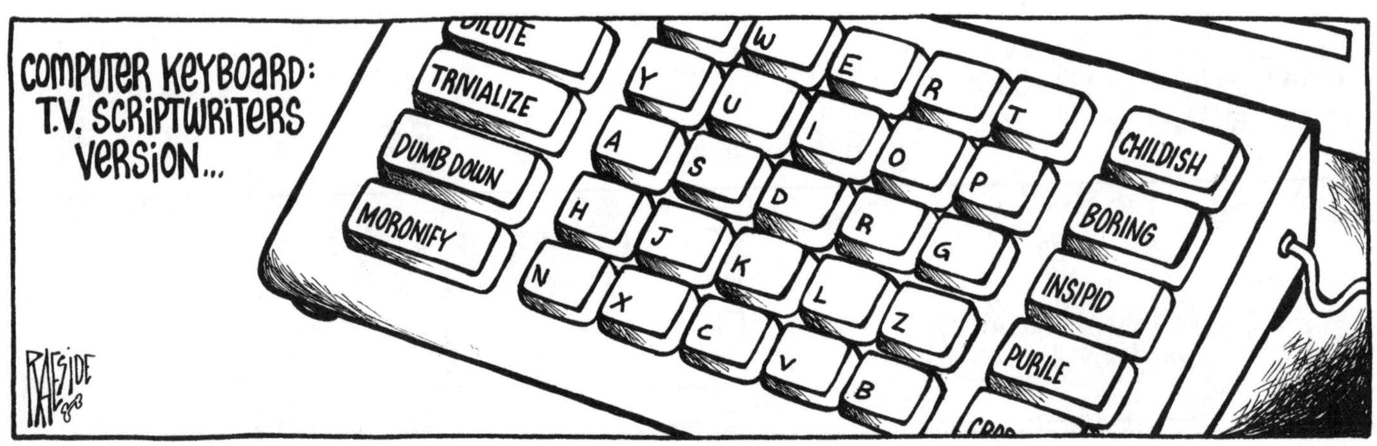
COMPUTER KEYBOARD:
T.V. SCRIPTWRITERS
VERSION...
TRIVIALIZE
DUMB DOWN
MORONIFY
Y
W
E
R
T
U
I
O
P
A
S
D
R
G
H
J
K
L
Z
N
X
C
V
B
CHILDISH
BORING
INSIPID
PURILE
RAESIDE

the OTHER COAST

SOME SAY THAT AGES AGO, INTELLIGENT BEINGS FROM ANOTHER PLANET VISITED EARTH...

THEY SHOWED US ADVANCED ENGINEERING TECHNIQUES, MATHEMATICS AND ASTROLOGY.

BUT IN MODERN TIMES, THEY SEEM TO HAVE LOST INTEREST IN US. WHY?

RAESIDE
COMING UP, FOUR EX-CHILD SITCOM STARS WRESTLE FOR CASH, IN A PIT OF WORMS.

BECAUSE THEY'RE INTELLIGENT?

JEEPERS, IT'S ALMOST IMPOSSIBLE TO DRILL THIS ICE FISHING HOLE. I WONDER WHAT'S UNDER THE ICE?
BLACKTOP?
P
3 HOURS MAXIMUM
RAESIDE

WORK BOOTS
THEY DON'T WORK. I GOT LAID OFF YESTERDAY.
RAESIDE

PSST. YOU WANNA BUY A WATCH, OR A CAMERA?

NICE. DO YOU TAKE CREDIT CARDS?
NOPE. JUST WATCHES AND CAMERAS.
RAESIDE

HOW'S THAT NEW SOFTWARE LOADING UP?
RAESIDE

...WITH FRENCH FRIES.
AH, YOU MEAN POMME FRITES.
MENU

RAESIDE
WHAT'S THE DIFFERENCE?
TWELVE DOLLARS.
MENU

RAESIDE
SLAM!
THAT'S IT! THE T.V. NETWORKS HAVE SUNK TO A NEW LOW!
THEY DIDN'T BUY ANY OF YOUR SCRIPTS?
HOLLYWOOD BOX OFFICE

THEY DID, BUT ONLY AFTER GOING THROUGH EVERYTHING I HAD IN MY BRIEFCASE.

GREAT! WHAT DID THEY TAKE?
YOUR SHOPPING LIST.

the OTHER COAST
RAESIDE

LOOK TOULOSE. RING NECKED MARSH DUCKS MIGRATING NORTH!

THEY'RE SO MAJESTIC IN FLIGHT.

PARK PRESERVES ARE GREAT FOR WILDLIFE VIEWING.

BIRDWATCHING WORKS UP A BIG APPETITE. LET'S HIT THE CONCESSION.

NICE SANDWICH. WHAT'S IN IT?
RING NECKED MARSH DUCK.

MISTER LEO'S FALL COLLECTION IS TURNING HEADS. COTTON AND SILK COMBOS JUST SCREAM ELEGANCE!

FASHION

PEASANT BLOUSES TRIMMED WITH SILK IS DEFINITELY THE 'IN' LOOK THIS YEAR.

WOW. THIS WRITER IS SO FASHION SAVVY, SO DEBONAIR!

RAESIDE

GAZPACCIO PUMPS AND LYCRA BELTS COMBINE TO GIVE THAT LIGHT AND BREEZY LOOK.

RAESIDE
COOL TATTOO. WHERE DID YOU GET IT FROM?
A JELLYFISH.

RAESIDE
AFTER YEARS OF BEING A WAITER, I FINALLY GOT MY BIG BREAK. I'VE LANDED A PART IN FAMED DIRECTOR FREDRICO VERMICELLI'S LATEST PICTURE.
MENU
THAT'S GREAT. WHAT ARE YOU PLAYING?
A WAITER.
MENU

THESE NEW T.V. REMOTES ARE SO DARN COMPLICATED. I HAVE NO IDEA WHAT THESE BUTTONS DO...
RAESIDE
CLICK! CLICK!
NOPE, THAT DOESN'T SEEM TO DO ANYTHING EITHER...
SLAM!
SLAM!

the OTHER COAST

RAESIDE
MAYBE YOU SHOULD GIVE UP SNOWBOARDING AND TAKE UP A LESS DANGEROUS SPORT, LIKE CYCLING.

VICKY, WHAT KIND OF BANK NOTE IS THIS?
THE NEW EURO.
10 EURO

INSTEAD OF MULTIPLE CURRENCIES, THE EUROPEANS HAVE ADOPTED ONE SINGLE CURRENCY.
10 EURO

LOUIGI'S
€
CHANGE
WHICH MEANS WE ONLY GET RIPPED OFF ONCE?
RAESIDE
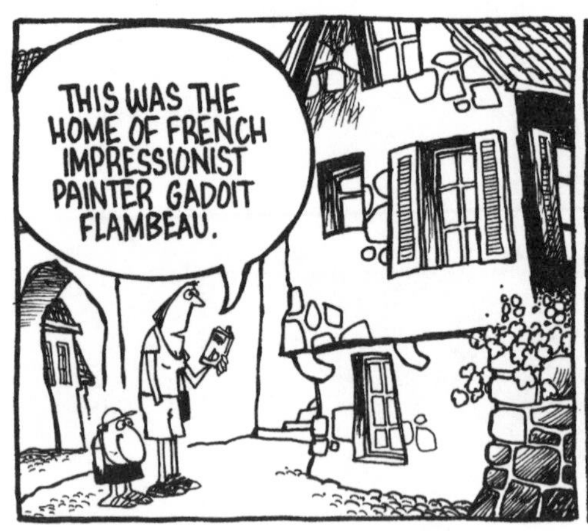
THIS WAS THE HOME OF FRENCH IMPRESSIONIST PAINTER GADOIT FLAMBEAU.

HE LIVED MOST OF HIS LIFE IN ABJECT POVERTY, REDUCED TO EATING TUBES OF PAINT.
GUIDE

RACKED BY TUBERCULOSIS, HE OVERDOSED ON BURNT UMBER AND CROISSANTS.

RAESIDE
KIND OF MAKES YOU MISS CINDERELLA'S CASTLE IN DISNEYLAND.
DID I MENTION THE LEPROSY?
GUIDE

LOOK AT THE SIZE OF THOSE YACHTS. WHO CAN AFFORD THESE FLOATING PALACES, ANYWAY?

RAESIDE
OUR PLUMBER.

FRENCH PHRASE BOOK
MENU
RAESIDE
CAFE PARIS

TOULOSE, WE'RE REALLY MOVING! WHAT'S THE SPEED LIMIT ON FRENCH FREEWAYS?
130 KILOMETERS PER HOUR.

RAESIDE
OF COURSE, THAT'S JUST A SUGGESTION.

CUSTOMS
ANYTHING TO DECLARE?

RAESIDE
I HAVEN'T DONE MY LAUNDRY IN TWO WEEKS.

the OTHER COAST
I LOVE CLIMBING. IT MAKES ME FEEL SO INVIGORATED.
RAESIDE

I WISH I COULD STAY UP IN THESE MOUNTAINS FOREVER.
LOOKS LIKE YOUR WISH JUST CAME TRUE.

SOMEONE JUST STOLE YOUR VEHICLE.

RAESIDE
CHAINSAW CARVINGS
NEXT LEFT

SALE

RAESIDE
AS PART OF MY MOVIE PROJECT, I'VE SET UP A HIDDEN CAMERA OUTSIDE.
WHAT'S IT FILMING?

LOOKS LIKE THE CONTENTS OF SOMONE'S PURSE.
I GUESS YOUR CAMERA WASN'T THAT WELL HIDDEN.

RAESIDE
TIMES ADVERTISER.

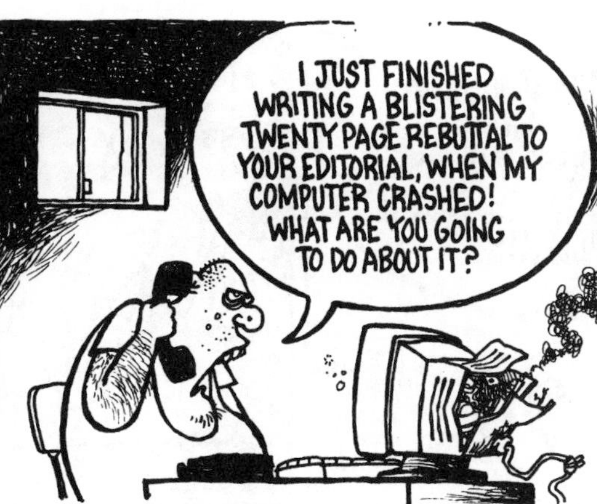
I JUST FINISHED WRITING A BLISTERING TWENTY PAGE REBUTTAL TO YOUR EDITORIAL, WHEN MY COMPUTER CRASHED! WHAT ARE YOU GOING TO DO ABOUT IT?

SEND A BOUQUET OF FLOWERS TO BILL GATES?

I CAN'T BELIEVE HOW EXPENSIVE DESIGNER ACCESSORIES HAVE BECOME.
I PICKED UP A NEW ALLIGATOR SKIN HANDBAG FOR TWO DOLLARS.
TWO DOLLARS FOR AN ALLIGATOR SKIN HANDBAG?
THE ALLIGATOR WAS RUN OVER BY AN OUTBOARD MOTOR.
RAESIDE

THE EDITING PROCESS:
SHRED
PUREE
CHOP
MINCE
RAESIDE

PEST CONTROL
PLUG IN THIS DEVICE AND IT EMITS A HIDEOUS HIGH-PITCHED NOISE THAT IS EXCRUTIATINGLY PAINFUL TO RODENTS.
THINK OF IT AS KARAOKE FOR RATS.
RAESIDE

the OTHER COAST
SNIFF SNIFF
SMELLS LIKE BARBEQUED STEAK.
SIZZLE
NO, CHICKEN.
POP!
SPARERIBS?
SIZZLE POP!
SALMON.
HEY TOULOSE, WHAT'S COOKING?
RAESIDE
BUGS.
SIZZLE
POP!

TEL
HELLO FRONT DESK? THERE'S A RAT STANDING AT THE FOOT OF MY BED. STARING AT ME.

TEL
HOW CAN I GET RID OF HIM?
RAESIDE
TIP HIM.
RULES

RAESIDE
A CHICAGO PUBLISHER WANTS TO TALK TO ME ABOUT MY NOVEL 'SLUG DETECTIVE' IN PERSON!

DO YOU REALIZE WHAT THIS MEANS?
THEY'VE RUN OUT OF FORM REJECTION LETTERS?

RAESIDE
JUST LOOK AT THOSE FANCY LAPTOP BAGS. LEATHER. STAINLESS STEEL. CANVAS...
COMPUTER
ACCESSORIES

EVERYTHING ABOUT THEM JUST SCREAMS EXPENSIVE LAPTOP.

YOU USE LAPTOPS A LOT?
NOPE, I STEAL THEM.

RAESIDE
SNOWBOARD STORE
WHOAH! CHECK OUT THIS WILD NEW SNOWBOARDING OUTFIT!
WHAT DO YOU CALL THESE AWESOME THREADS, MAN?
JUST LOOK AT THOSE EARTH TONES AND LIVED-IN LOOK!
MY DIRTY LAUNDRY.

NATIVES IN THE ARCTIC HAVE OVER 40 WORDS FOR WINTER CONDITIONS:
AKKILOKIPOK.
RAESIDE
...DRIVERS HAVE SLIGHTLY LESS:
JERK!
MORON!

ROCKET SCIENTIST PICNICS...
10...9...8...7...6...
RAESIDE

the OTHER COAST
SNIFF SNIFF
OH OOH...

UH, MISTER GRABBIT? THERE'S SOMETHING I NEED TO TELL YOU.

LARRY, YOU CAN'T JUST BARGE IN HERE EVERY TIME YOU GET SOME SCATTERED IDEA.

IF EVERY MINION CAME INTO MY OFFICE BLURTING OUT RANDOM THOUGHTS, THIS COMPANY WOULD DESCEND INTO TOTAL ANARCHY!
RAESIDE

GO BACK TO YOUR CUBICLE, FOLLOW OFFICE PROCEDURE AND EMAIL ME A MEMO!

The building is on fire.

SNACKS
RAESIDE

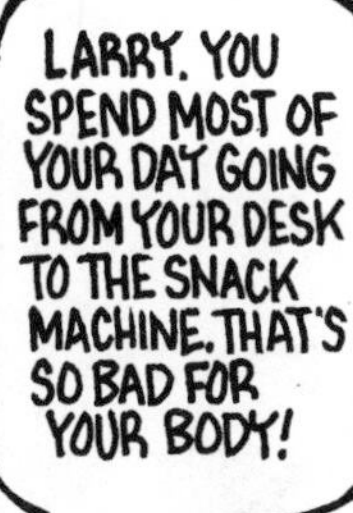
LARRY. YOU SPEND MOST OF YOUR DAY GOING FROM YOUR DESK TO THE SNACK MACHINE. THAT'S SO BAD FOR YOUR BODY!

SNACKS

HELLO TOULOSE? I'VE GOT YOUR LATEST SCRIPT IN FRONT OF ME. IT HAS THE 'O' WORD WRITTEN ALL OVER IT, MAN.
HOLLYWOO
OSCAR?

RAESIDE
OBNOXIOUS.
NO KIDDING! WHEN DO THEY GIVE OUT THAT AWARD?

AS A T.V. WEATHER FORECASTER, I HAVE ACCESS TO SOPHISTICATED COMPUTER PROJECTIONS AND DATA.
..AND I STILL CAN'T GET IT RIGHT.
THAT'S NOTHING.

OH? WHAT'S YOUR PROFESSION?
STOCK ANALYST.
RAESIDE

I THINK I'M ADDICTED TO SPECIALTY CABLE CHANNELS. I JUST SPENT THE ENTIRE WEEKEND WATCHING OLD COLUMBO RE-RUNS.
SO WHAT. IT WAS A GREAT SERIES.

RAESIDE
...IN TURKISH.
I'LL CALL THE BETTY FORD CLINIC.

RAESIDE
I WANT TO STOP IN AND SEE A BUDDY WHO'S RECOVERING FROM AN ACCIDENT ON THE SKI HILL.
HOSPITAL
EMERGENCY

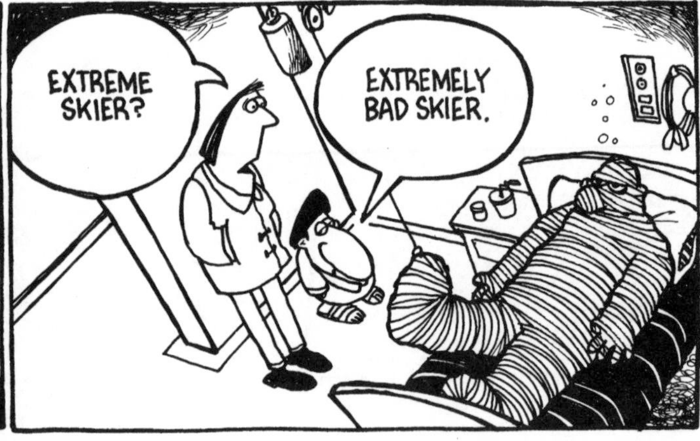
EXTREME SKIER?
EXTREMELY BAD SKIER.

HEH, HEH. NOW THAT WINTER IS HERE, WE DON'T HAVE TO ENDURE THOSE NOISY PERSONAL WATER CRAFT.

RAESIDE
BZZZAAAAWW

the OTHER COAST
TOULOSE! TIME FOR YOU TO SAVE THE PLANET!
I WANT YOU TO TAKE OUR RECYCLABLES TO THE RECYCLING DEPOT.
BOTTLES IN THE GREEN BIN. TINS IN THE BLUE BIN. NEWSPAPERS IN THE RED BIN.
YEAH, YEAH.
RAESIDE
BOTTLES IN THE BLUE BIN...NO, GREEN BIN. NO. GREEN IS FOR TINS... NO...

TURN LEFT AT THE YELLOW HOUSE... WHAT KIND OF DIRECTIONS ARE THESE? WE'RE COLORBLIND!
RAESIDE

YOU'RE GOING HUNTING WITH BOB? KILLING ANIMALS IS BARBARIC!
WHAT ABOUT THAT HAMBURGER YOU ATE LAST WEEK?
IT WAS HIT BY A CAR!
RAESIDE

RAESIDE
THEY MAY LOOK ALIKE, BUT THE REAL BUSH DOESN'T SMELL OF STALE BEER AND CIGARS.
BUSH
HUNTER

RAESIDE
AAH YES. TREKKING INTO THE WILDERNESS TO HUNT WILD GAME, JUST LIKE MY ANCESTORS.

BOB, YOUR ANCESTORS DIDN'T DRIVE A LUXURY SUV.

HEY, THIS IS YOUR BASIC MODEL, NO MOONROOF.
YOU ARE A TRUE PIONEER.

CHIP! CHIP!
BE ALERT TO THE SOUNDS OF THE WILDERNESS. THAT'S A CHIPMUNK...

TOK! TOK!
THAT'S A WOODPECKER.

CRASH!
...TINKLE.

RAESIDE
...AND THAT'S SOMEBODY BREAKING INTO YOUR SUV.

WE'VE BEEN HIDING IN THESE BUSHES FOR HOURS WITHOUT SEEING ANY WILDLIFE.

NO PROBLEM, I'LL ATTRACT 'EM.

RAESIDE
I HAD MY CELLPHONE PROGRAMMED...

...TO RING THE THEME SONG FROM 'BORN FREE.'
WE'LL BE STAMPEDED.

the OTHER COAST
Z

Z
Z
Z
HMM. I DON'T REMEMBER THIS SANDBAR BEING ON THE CHARTS.

AAH VICKY, NOTHING LIKE A HOT TUB TO SOAK YOUR CARES AWAY.

FORGET ABOUT RECESSION, GLOBAL CONFLICT, INTEREST RATES...

RAESIDE
GLOBAL WARMING.

BOB, GLADYS. YOU LIVE IN A KNOWN EARTHQUAKE ZONE. HAVE YOU EARTHQUAKE-PROOFED THE HOT TUB?
GIMBALLED DRINK HOLDERS.
RAESIDE

...CAN CAUSE LIGHT HEADEDNESS, EUPHORIA, LETHARGY AND INCREASED APPETITE.

RAESIDE
WHAT IS THAT DRUG?
I DUNNO, BUT IT'S WORTH TAKING JUST FOR THE SIDE EFFECTS.

NEXT TIME WE PIT MAN AGAINST COMPUTER, LET'S STICK WITH CHESS.
RAESIDE

BANK
OCCUPATION?
RAESIDE

I WRITE SCRIPTS FOR INTELLIGENT AND THOUGHTFUL TELEVISION SHOWS.
UNEMPLOYED.

RAESIDE
24 hr NEWS
DOW
8,709
ONLINE POLL: 36%
UN SPOKESPERSON ANNOUNCES
ANCE OF SHOWS LOW 61 HIGH 80-TUE
03
COMING UP IN THE NEXT HOUR, IS THERE SUCH A THING AS TOO MUCH INFORMATION?

the OTHER COAST
BANANA STRETCH.
RAESIDE

SCRITCH
SCRATCH
SCRITCH

HAK!

BURRRP!

POOT!

DO YOU EVER GET THE FEELING DOGS ARE JUST REINCARNATED MEN?
Z

RAESIDE
VICKY, WHAT DO YOU THINK MY CHANCES ARE OF GETTING A REFUND ON THAT ANGER MANAGEMENT COURSE?

TOULOSE, YOU GOT A 100 DOLLAR PHOTO RADAR TICKET...
PLUS A 50 DOLLAR FINE FOR PUBLIC INDECENCY.
RAESIDE
PUBLIC INDECENCY?!
YOU WERE SNAPPED WHILE PICKING YOUR NOSE.

IF MICHELANGELO WAS A NEWSPAPER CARTOONIST:
RAESIDE
NICE FRESCOES. TOO BAD THEY'LL BE WRAPPING FISH TOMORROW.

RAESIDE
COCKROACH NURSING HOME
POOR OLD FRANK. HE'S NEVER BEEN THE SAME SINCE HE WAS HIT BY THAT SIZE FOURTEEN LOAFER.

ATE 15
52
PLEASE DON'T BE SITTING NEXT TO ME.
PLEASE DON'T BE SITTING NEXT TO ME.
PLEASE DON'T BE SITTING NEXT TO ME.
PLEASE DON'T BE SITTING NEXT TO ME.
RAESIDE

CIGAR LOUNGE
CAN I GET YOU GENTLEMEN ANYTHING? VODKA?.. GIN?.. OXYGEN?
RAESIDE

the OTHER COAST
THIS HAS BEEN A FABULOUS EVENING.

I HAD A BEER, CHAMPAGNE, A WINE COOLER, CRANBERRY COCKTAIL... WHAT ELSE COULD I NEED?
RAESIDE

A BATHROOM?
SOMEBODY SHOOT DOWN THIS BALLOON!

HOW WHITE WATER KYAKERS TRAIN:
SOAP
WASH
RINSE

STOP THE LOGGING
O.K. O.K. YOU WIN! WE GIVE UP.

HAH! WAS IT MY PERSISTENCE THAT DROVE YOU OFF?

NOPE. YOUR SMELL.

TRANSITION HOUSE -FOR- FAILED DOT COMS
HUH! THAT'S NOTHIN'! BY THE TIME WE FOLDED, WE'D BURNED THROUGH THIS MUCH VENTURE CAPITAL!

ACRES OF BEDS, CARS, FREEZERS, T.V.S. THESE BIG-BOX MEGASTORES ARE JUST TOO DARN HUGE!
AISLE 178
WHATEVER HAPPENED TO THE OLD FASHIONED MOM AND POP STORE?
RAESIDE
AISLE 239.
HI

a HIGHLY TRAINED AVALANCHE RESCUE DOG, REX STILL RETAINED CERTAIN 'DOGGY' TRAITS...
O.K. LET'S GET THIS STRAIGHT. YOU DUG THE SKIIER OUT, THEN REBURIED HIM, BUT YOU DON'T REMEMBER WHERE...
RAESIDE

U.V. RADIATION? NAH, THESE DAYS I'M MORE CONCERNED ABOUT CELLPHONE RADIATION.
RAESIDE

the OTHER COAST
YOU'LL LOVE THIS RESTAURANT TOULOSE.
the Tasty TERMITE

WORMS, COCKROACHES, TERMITES, ANTS... VICKY, WHAT KIND OF MENU IS THIS?
MENU
IN SOME COUNTRIES THESE ARE CONSIDERED DELICACIES. BESIDES, THEY'RE VERY NUTRITIOUS.
RAESIDE
WHAT DO CANDIED CRICKETS TASTE LIKE?
SIMILAR TO SAUTÉED SLUGS.
CAN I HAVE FRIES WITH THAT?

WHY OCTOPI DON'T SKI...
SKI BOOTS
RAESIDE

THIS IS AN '87! WHAT ARE YOU TRYING TO DO, POISON ME?
BRANDY
WHEN OENOPHILES GET LOST IN THE MOUNTAINS:
RAESIDE

I LOVE COMING UP TO THE MOUNTAINS TO GET AWAY FROM IT ALL.
LODGE
INTERNET Café
FAX
ATM
CELLPHONES
RAESIDE

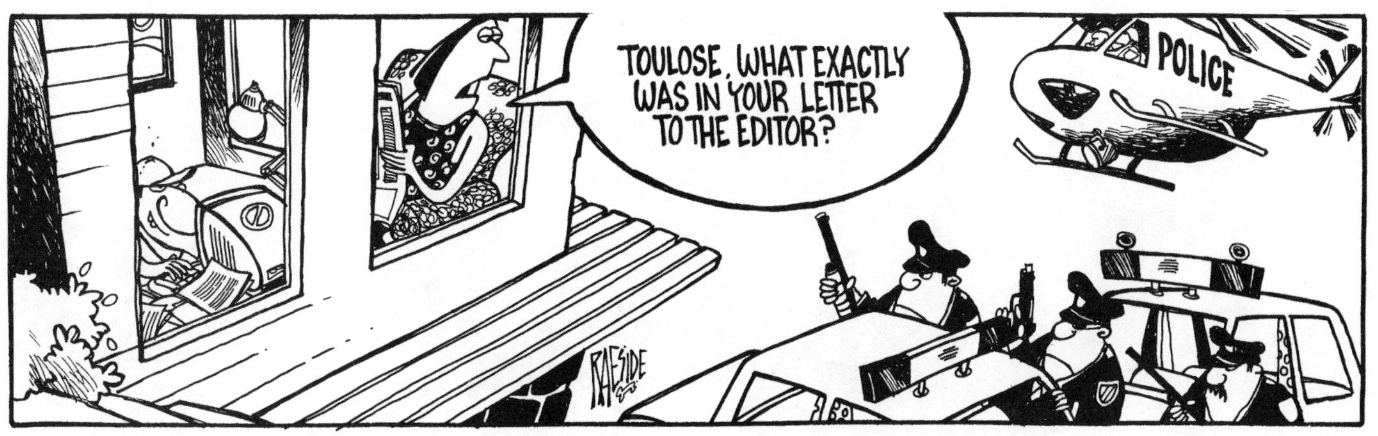
TOULOSE, WHAT EXACTLY WAS IN YOUR LETTER TO THE EDITOR?
POLICE
RAESIDE

CLASSIC SCENARIO. TOO MANY 'FRIDGE MAGNETS, SOMEONE WITH A STEEL PLATE IN HIS HEAD GETS TOO CLOSE...
RAESIDE

DESPITE RUSTY'S CLAIM THAT HE WAS NOWHERE NEAR THE BEDROOM, THIS PHOTO CLEARLY SHOWS A SUSPICIOUS INDENTATION ON THE BEDSPREAD...
RAESIDE

the OTHER COAST
LOOK AT THAT. ONE OF NATURE'S MOST EFFICIENT PREDATORS.

THEY'RE RUTHLESS AND DEADLY. YOU'D NEVER WANT TO ENCOUNTER A SCHOOL OF THEM WHEN THEY'RE IN A FEEDING FRENZY.

RAESIDE.
SO, HOW LONG HAS YOUR LAWYER BEEN MOONLIGHTING AT THE AQUARIUM?

IT'S FASCINATING TO SEE WHAT WASHES UP ON THE SHORE AFTER A BIG STORM.
RAESIDE

FOR EXAMPLE, LOOK AT THAT MOTTLED BLOB, LYING ON THE BEACH OVER THERE.

THAT'S LARRY IN A SPEEDO.

DOC, WHICH SHOTS SHOULD I GET BEFORE I GO ON HOLIDAY?
DEPENDS ON WHERE YOU'RE GOING.

A CARIBBEAN RESORT CALLED DYSENTERY REEF.
RAESIDE

BEND OVER.

MA'AM? I'LL HAVE TO ASK YOU TO PUT YOUR EXCESS BAGGAGE IN THE OVERHEAD BIN.

RAESIDE

ARRIV
HOW LONG IS THE RIDE INTO TOWN?
BEATS ME. NONE OF OUR CABS HAVE EVER MADE IT THAT FAR.
TAXI
CAB STAND
RAESIDE

THIS PLACE CAN'T BE TOO BAD TOULOSE. IT'S RECOMMENDED AS A FAMILY RESORT.
GUIDE
THE ADDAMS FAMILY?
RAESIDE

RAESIDE
BUT ON THE PHONE YOU SAID YOU WERE 'STEPS FROM THE BEACH.'
DYSENTERY REEF
YOU NEVER ASKED HOW MANY STEPS.

the OTHER COAST
POLICE ARE CLOSING IN ON THE STOLEN VEHICLE...
SPEEDS IN THIS CHASE HAVE CLOCKED IN AT OVER 100 MILES AN HOUR!
WHOOAH! THE SUSPECT CAR JUST CLIPPED A LIGHT POLE!
WHAT ARE YOU WATCHING TOULOSE?
A REAL LIFE POLICE PURSUIT, VICKY.
WELL HOW'S THIS FOR REAL LIFE? OUR CAR HAS BEEN STOLEN OUT OF THE DRIVEWAY.
I THOUGHT THAT CAR LOOKED FAMILIAR.

WOW. CHANGES ARE SO DRAMATIC ON A TROPICAL ISLAND...
RAESIDE

THE WEATHER, THE SUNSETS, THE ATMOSPHERE.

THE GOVERNMENT.
THAT EXPLAINS THE TANK PARKED IN THE LOBBY.

RAT A TAT TAT TAT TAT TAT
BOOM! BANG BANG

IT STOPPED. THE REVOLUTION MUST BE OVER.
RAESIDE

NAH. THOSE WERE JUST THE PRIMARIES.

IN A REVOLUTION, THE FIRST TO GO IS THE T.V. STATION.
I'LL SEE IF THEY'RE STILL ON AIR.

COMING UP, BARBARA WALTERS INTERVIEWS ANNA NICOLE SMITH...

RAESIDE
WHAT ARE YOU WAITING FOR? THE T.V. STATION IS THAT WAY!

DESPITE THE REVOLUTION AND CHAOS, WE'RE STILL ABLE TO GET FRESH FRUIT DELIVERED.
CRUNCH!
TOULOSE, HOW COME THIS PINEAPPLE IS SO HARD?
BECAUSE IT'S A GRENADE.
RAESIDE

LOOK VICKY. A BUNCH OF SOLDIERS JUST COMMANDEERED A CAR.
THERE MUST BE 20 GUYS PACKED INTO THAT SUB COMPACT.

HEH HEH. THEY JUST DROVE INTO A DITCH. WHAT A HOOT!
BE MORE OF A HOOT IF THEY WEREN'T DRIVING OUR RENTAL CAR.
RAESIDE

SOLDIERS AND TANKS IN THE STREETS. WE'RE TRAPPED IN OUR ROOM VICKY.

WE'RE ALSO OUT OF ICE.
RAESIDE

ICE

the OTHER COAST
BZZZAWWW!

BZZZAWW!

BZZZAWW!

RAESIDE
HELLO? WHY ARE YOU CLEARING THIS LAND?

THIS IS THE FUTURE SITE OF A FOREST APPRECIATION CENTER.
NICE VIEW OF THE STUMPS.

CHECK OUT
YOU'RE BEING BILLED FIVE NIGHTS GARDEN VIEW AND ONE NIGHT OCEAN VIEW.
SINCE WHEN DID OUR ROOM HAVE AN OCEAN VIEW?
SINCE AN ARTILLERY ROUND TOOK OUT THE BACK WALL.
RAESIDE

WHERE THAT ONE MISSING SOCK GOES...
LAUNDR
RAESIDE

SIMON? WHAT'S A VEGAN DOING WEARING A BUCKSKIN JACKET?
THIS IS KANGAROO HIDE. MADE ONLY FROM KANGAROOS NATURALLY CULLED FROM THE HERD.
HEY, IT EVEN HAS A COOL LOGO ON THE BACK.
THAT'S THE IMPRESSION LEFT BY THE FRONT GRILLE OF A FORD PICKUP.
RAESIDE

WORKING OUT IS VERY IMPORTANT FOR ME...

I WANT TO MAINTAIN MY TRIM AND LITHE FIGURE.

GYM
RAESIDE

THE DISADVANTAGE TO BEING THE LAST ONE UP TO THE SALAD BAR:
SALAD BAR
POTATO SALAD
DRESSING
BREAD ROLLS
ICE
PICKLED PIG EARS
BEEF
CARROTS
RAESIDE

DISCOUNT WHALE WATCHING TOURS:
THERE'S ONE.
SEE THE WHALES
CHEAPY
RAESIDE

the OTHER COAST
COMING UP, CELEBRITY ARM WRESTLING FROM TORONTO...
AARGH! I'M SICK OF WATCHING TRASH ON BASIC CABLE!
A SATELLITE DISH WILL PUT ME IN TOUCH WITH QUALITY T.V. PROGRAMMING FROM AROUND THE WORLD.
HEH HEH... SIX HUNDRED CHANNELS OF CHOICE.
COMING UP, CELEBRITY ARM WRESTLING FROM OSLO...

TROUBLE BREWING AT THE SIMIAN SINGLES BAR:
TAKE YOUR HANDS OFF ME, YOU DIRTY APE!
RAESIDE

MORE EVIDENCE PRO WRESTLING IS STAGED:
GRUNT SNARL
GRUNT
RAESIDE

WHY YES, LARRY IS OUR SPECIALIST IN PLUMBING REPAIRS. WHY DO YOU ASK?
RAESIDE

BAESIDE
IT MUST BE SUMMER. I'VE JUST SEEN MY FIRST IRATE MOTORIST STUCK BEHIND US.

THERE'S A SAYING THAT THE UPS AND DOWNS OF OUR ECONOMY ARE REFLECTED IN GIRL'S HEMLINES.
BAESIDE
WE'RE DOOMED.

MUSIC THERAPY IN 2063:
OKAAY. NOW LET'S TRY SOMETHING FROM NINE INCH NAILS.
BAESIDE

the OTHER COAST
SWIM WITH THE DOLPHINS
OPEN TODAY!

LARGE POINTY FIN ON THE BACK?
UH HUH.
MARINE LIFE

LONG ROW OF SHARP TEETH?
OH YEAH.
MARINE LIFE

VORACIOUS APPETITE?
MY GOODNESS, YES.
MARINE LIFE

SO THAT DEFINITELY IS A SHARK?
NO QUESTION.
RAESIDE

DARN. I COULD HAVE SWORN WE'D BOUGHT DOLPHINS.
URP!

LARRY, I THOUGHT YOU WERE ON A CELEBRITY DIET.
I AM. THE ORSON WELLES DIET.
RAESIDE

DOG RESTAURANTS:
RAESIDE
AND HERE'S YOUR ...OOPS, SORRY, THE ALPHA DOG AT TABLE TWENTY ONE GOT IT FIRST.

HEY VICKY, I JUST GOT MY MBA DIPLOMA! I WENT THE FASTRACK ROUTE.
HOW LONG DID IT TAKE YOU LARRY?
RAESIDE
THIRTY FIVE SECONDS.
GOTTA LOVE HIGH SPEED INTERNET.

GAS
ARE YOUR RESTROOMS CLEAN?
ARE YOUR SHOTS UP TO DATE?
MEN
RAESIDE

CHAINING MYSELF TO A TREE TO STOP THE LOGGING IS AS GREEN AS IT GETS.
WASN'T THAT CHAIN MADE IN AN ASIAN SWEATSHOP?

IT WAS AN ORGANIC SWEATSHOP!
RAESIDE

ERNIE THE EMBEZZLER! HOW WAS PRISON?
LIKE I NEVER LEFT THE OFFICE.

RAESIDE
YOU'RE KIDDING.
THE ENTIRE BOARD OF DIRECTORS WAS SENT UP WITH ME.

the OTHER COAST
UGH. THIS ATTIC NEEDS ORGANIZING.

SHOOOK! THUMP! THUMP!

RAESIDE

HEY TOULOSE, I FOUND YOUR FAMILY PHOTO ALBUM.
PHOTO

WOO! THAT IS ONE UGLY FAMILY DOG!
THAT'S ME WHEN I WAS THREE.
PHOTO

THE ADVANTAGE TO BEING A PANDA BEAR:

ONCE AGAIN, DR. FRANKENSTEIN WAS WINNING HEARTS AND MINDS...
RAESIDE

RAESIDE
EEEAARGH! IT'S THE SWAMP CREATURE!
SOMEBODY FORGOT TO PUT CHLORINE IN THE HOT TUB.

WINE FESTIV
RAESIDE
EXCELLENT WINE. I JUST BOUGHT FIFTY CASES CHECK OUT THEIR MERLOT. BUT HURRY, CASES ARE LIMITED.
VICKY, WHAT'S THE DIFFERENCE BETWEEN A WINE CONNOISEUR AND A WINO?
ABOUT TWENTY BUCKS A BOTTLE.

the OTHER COAST
AAH...THIS TREE BRINGS BACK MEMORIES. I CARVED MY INITIALS INTO ITS TRUNK AND NAILED A TREE FORT INTO ITS BRANCHES.

RAESIDE
THUD!

PAYBACK.

RAESIDE
EVER WONDERED HOW THEY COME UP WITH ALL THOSE INTERESTING WINE LABELS?

WHY WOULD THEY DESIGN A LABEL THAT FEATURES AN OLD POSSUM?
BECAUSE IT TASTES LIKE OLD POSSUM.
PFFT!

RAESIDE
WINE FESTIVAL
IF YOU PURCHASE OVER TEN CASES, YOU'RE ELIGIBLE TO WIN A FREE TRIP.
PINOT NOIR

COOL. WHERE TO?
THE BETTY FORD CLINIC.
PINOT NOIR

RAESIDE
WINE FESTIVALS ARE SOOO BORING. AT LEAST THEY GOT SNACKS.

CHEW
CHEW CHEW
CHEW
CH

YECH! WHAT DO YOU CALL THESE VILE SNACKS?
CORKS.
P-TOO!

MMM. WHAT WOULD YOU PAIR WITH THIS WINE?
MEAT, OR WILD GAME.

VERY NICE. WHAT WOULD YOU PAIR WITH THIS?
POULTRY, OR FISH.

AND WHAT WOULD YOU PAIR WITH THIS WINE?
ASPIRIN.
RAESIDE

RAESIDE
HEY, I LIKE THIS WINE VICKY.
TOULOSE, YOU DON'T DRINK THE WINE, YOU TASTE IT, THEN SPIT IT OUT...

SPIT

WINE FEST
INTO A BUCKET, NOT SOMEONE'S SHOE.

I LOVE HOW YOU'VE DECORATED YOUR OFFICE... EARLY CALIFORNIA? LATE VICTORIAN?
RECENT REJECTION LETTERS.
RAESIDE

the OTHER COAST
ONLY 38 SHOPPING DAYS UNTIL XMAS!

SALE!

NO MORE HOLIDAY SHOPPING MAYHEM FOR ME. I'M CATALOGUE SHOPPING THIS YEAR.
RAESIDE

I'LL PICK UP THE CATALOGUES AT THE MALL IN A QUIET AND DIGNIFIED MANNER.
SMART.

MALL
BACK IN FIVE.

CATALOGUES

I'M NOT TAKING ANY CHANCES. I'M WEARING A SURGICAL MASK...

I DON'T TOUCH ANYTHING WITHOUT WEARING GLOVES...
OPEN

COFFEE
HEH HEH. NO COLD BUG IS GETTING ME THIS YEAR.
A-A-A CHOO!

I'M GOING TO THE DRUG STORE TO GET SOMETHING FOR YOUR COLD.
DON'T FORGET TO TELL THE PHARMACIST ALL MY SYMPTOMS!

COUGH, SNIFFLES, SNEEZING AND A CONSTANT IRRITATING WHINE.
PHARMACY

TOULOSE, I'M GOING TO MAKE YOU MY GREAT GRANDMOTHER'S COLD REMEDY...

THE ORIGINAL RECIPE HAS BEEN IN MY FAMILY FOR GENERATIONS.

'COURSE, I HAD TO SUBSTITUTE RAW PORK LIVER FOR PICKLED OX BRAINS.

I'LL CHECK THE INTERNET FOR FOR COLD REMEDIES.
LOOK UP MY SYMPTOMS VICKY.

RUNNY NOSE, FEVER. HEADACHE, SORE THROAT, WATERY EYES, SNEEZING, RAZOR BURN, WARTS...

WHAT DID THEY SUGGEST?
EARPLUGS.
RAESIDE

DOCTOR, I'VE TRIED EVERYTHING. ANTIBIOTICS, PAINKILLERS, POULTICES... I STILL CAN'T GET TOULOSE OUT OF BED.
RAESIDE

TRY DISCONNECTING THE CABLE.
COMING UP ON OPRAH...

VICKY, I FEEL BETTER! BRING ME MY COMPUTER, I'M GOING TO WORK.

I GOTTA GET A LAPTOP.
RAESIDE

the OTHER COAST

YOU'LL LOVE THIS, TOULOSE. CHEF KOBAYASHI-SAN CAN MAKE ANYTHING TASTE DELICIOUS.
MY FAVOURITE... HACHIMAKI ROLL.
GEE...WHAT IS IT, VICKY?
TASTE IT, YOU'LL LOVE IT.
IT'S A HEADBAND IN RICE.
WHAT DID I TELL YOU? HE'S A GENIUS!

HOW GUYS BUY SWIMSUITS:
MEN'S L
MEN'S XL
IT'LL HANG LIKE A TENT, MAKE YOUR BUTT LOOK ENORMOUS AND ACCENTUATE YOUR BEER GUT.
PAM
I'LL TAKE TWO.
RAESIDE

WHY DOGS MAKE LOUSY POKER PLAYERS:
THUMPA THUMPA THUMP
RAESIDE

STICIDE
THIS ROACH MOTEL COSTS TWICE WHAT THIS ONE COSTS. HOW COME?
IT HAS COMPLIMENTARY COFFEE.
RAESIDE

HEY VICKY, THESPIAN BOB IS BACK ON T.V.
YOU'RE KIDDING! HE HASN'T BEEN IN A PRIME TIME DRAMA IN YEARS.
ACTUALLY, IT'S MORE OF A CURRENT AFFAIRS PROGRAM.

ACTION NEWS 10
DON'T JUMP BEFORE I GET A REMOTE MIKE ON YOU.

COME ON DOWN THESPIAN BOB. THINGS CAN'T REALLY BE THAT BAD.
I'M A CLASSICALLY TRAINED BROADWAY ACTOR SURROUNDED BY A SEA OF LOW-BROW REALITY T.V. PROGRAMS.

JUMP.

DESPITE THE EFFORTS OF POLICE, THE JUMPER REFUSES TO COME DOWN.
CLICK

THIS IS SICK. EVERY NETWORK IS COVERING THESPIAN BOB ON THE BRIDGE.
CLICK
CLICK

HEY, THE FASHION CHANNEL. GOOD. WHOLESOME FARE.
COORDINATING YOUR WARDROBE...

OH MY. IF I WORE THAT SWEATER WITH THOSE SHOES, I'D JUMP TOO.

the OTHER COAST
CHEW CHEW
GOBBLE SCARF CHO
SLOOORP!

URP
THE END

GREAT MOVIE, TOULOSE.

RAESIDE

WHAT ARE YOU WAITING FOR? LET'S GO.
CAN'T. I'M STUCK TO THE FLOOR.

THESPIAN BOB, A PRODUCER OF A PRIME TIME SERIES SAW YOU ON THE NEWS AND THINKS YOU'D BE PERFECT FOR A LEAD ROLE.

FANTASTIC! CSI MIAMI? THE SOPRANOS?
COPS.

HANG TIGHT. WE'VE GOT AN EXPERT IN GETTING FOLKS DOWN FROM HIGH PLACES, ON HIS WAY.
OH. WHAT'S HIS BACKGROUND?

SKEET SHOOTING.

THESPIAN BOB CLIMBED DOWN OFF THE BRIDGE AND TURNED HIS LIFE AROUND WITH HELP FROM A PROFESSIONAL.
SHRINK?

AGENT.
BRIDGE DRAMA A NOVEL BY THESPIAN BOB
THESPIAN B
ACTION FI
THESPIAN BOB BRIDGE TV SERIES
DVD

RAESIDE 8-3
YOU'RE GOING TO THE WRITER'S CONFERENCE TOULOSE?
YEP. TWO HUNDRED WRITERS IN A HOTEL FOR TWO DAYS. PBS WILL BE FILMING IT TOO.
MIDDLE-AGED HACKS GONE WILD.
TAXI

AL, IT'S SO GOOD TO SEE YOU!
JUDY, YOU LOOK TERRIFIC!
TOULOSE, I JUST LOVE YOUR WORK.
C'MON BOB, YOU'RE THE MAN!

RAESIDE 8-3
OILY LITTLE CREEP.
HAS SHE EVER AGED.
TALENTLESS BUM.
RANK AMATEUR.

RAESIDE 8-3
HELLO, MY NAME IS MIKE
TODAY'S SEMINARS
9 AM: SURVIVING A HANGOVER.
11 AM: THE MECHANICS OF A HANGOVER.
2 PM: MAKING MONEY FROM A HANGOVER.

the OTHER COAST

CHOMP!

CHOMP CHOMP CHO

RAESIDE

I HATE IT WHEN
YOUR RELATIVES
COME TO VISIT.

RAESIDE 8-8
DUE TO THE FACT NOBODY HAS PAID THEIR DUES FOR THREE YEARS, THE SOCIETY IS FLAT BROKE.
SOCIETY OF WRITE
THE GOOD NEWS IS, WE'RE NOW ELIGIBLE FOR FOOD STAMPS.
CLAP CLAP
CLAP CLAP

RAESIDE 8-8
HOW WAS THE WRITER'S CONVENTION, TOULOSE?
FABULOUS! I EVEN WALKED AWAY WITH A TROPHY.
SOME TROPHY. IT LOOKS LIKE A BEDSIDE LAMP.
IF THE HOTEL SHOULD CALL, YOU NEVER HEARD OF ME.

The FiRST SWiM-UP BaR:
RAESIDE 8-8

CHICKEN SOUP
FOR THE SOUL
PUBLISHING
THERE'S SOMEONE ON THE PHONE WHO SAYS OUR BOOKS SUCK.
WHO IS IT?
THE CHICKEN.
RAESIDE

DOG FAMILY TREES:
SON
MOM
POSSIBLE DAD
COULD BE HIM
OR HIM
NOT OUT OF THE QUESTION
RAESIDE

I WON 150 MILLION IN THE LOTTERY, YET I CAN'T BRING MYSELF TO QUIT MY JOB AT THE GAS STATION. WHY?
YOU'RE AN IDIOT.
RAESIDE

the OTHER COAST

THUMP! THUMP!
TOULOSE, WAKE UP! A RACCOON IS ON THE ROOF TRYING TO GET INTO THE ATTIC.

GRUMBLE MUMBLE GRUMBLE

BEAT IT, YOU VARMINT.

RAESIDE

IF YOU PROMISE NOT TO HOG THE COMFORTER, YOU CAN STAY.

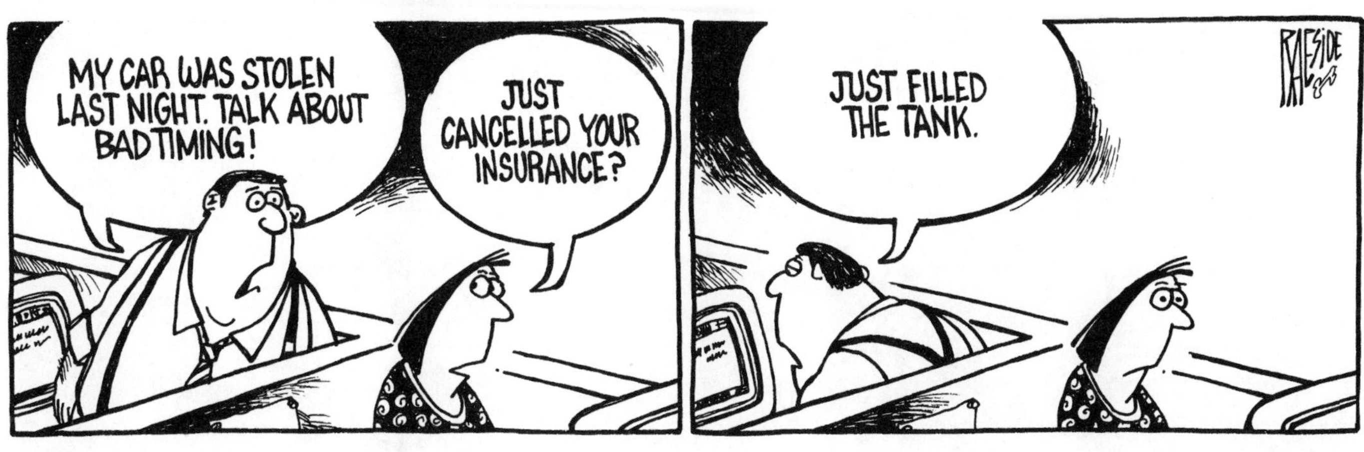
MY CAR WAS STOLEN LAST NIGHT. TALK ABOUT BAD TIMING!
JUST CANCELLED YOUR INSURANCE?
JUST FILLED THE TANK.
RAESIDE

WHAT ARE WE LISTENING TO?
A READING OF THE LATE WILF BUCHAN'S LOST POEMS.

O SLUDGE. YOU ARE SO SLUDGEY. I WISH I WAS A WORM...

RAESIDE
THEY WEREN'T LOST, THEY WERE THROWN OUT.

IT MUST BE GREAT TO OWN A BOAT.
BOATING IS A RICH MAN'S SPORT.
AVRIO

MY MARINA OWNER IS RICH.
MY MECHANIC IS RICH.
MY MARINE SUPPLY STORE OWNER IS RICH...
RAESIDE

RAESIDE
HAPPENS EVERY TIME... RUSTY INVITES GUESTS OVER FOR DINNER, THEN FORGETS WHERE HE BURIED IT.

CONSTRUCTION ZONE
LUCKY! THAT BRICK JUST BARELY MISSED ME!
THAT'S A GOOD OMEN, TOULOSE. YOU SHOULD BUY A LOTTERY TICKET.

RAESIDE
OPEN
LOTTE
WIN!
5.5

CONCESSION
AAAH. THE MAGIC OF THE CINEMA.
RAESIDE

THE SPECIAL EFFECTS. THE ELABORATE STUNTS.
HOW FAST A FIFTY DISAPPEARS.

the OTHER COAST
SNOB HILL
GOLF COURSE

RING!
RAESIDE

IT·S NIKE. THEY'LL PAY YOU MILLION BUCKS IF YOU DON·T WEAR THEIR GEAR.